A
Powerful
Ascent

How the power to restart changes the way we lead, act and feel

Carol A. Nero

Copyright © by Carol A. Nero 2022. All rights reserved.

Before this document is duplicated or reproduced in any manner, the publisher's consent must be gained. Therefore, the contents within can neither be stored electronically, transferred, nor kept in a database. Neither in Part nor full can the document be copied, scanned, faxed, or retained without approval from the publisher or creator.

Table of Contents

The science of exposure

Accepting ourselves

The quake

The uprising

The science of exposure

Instability is not Vulnerability. Have you heard someone talk about a problem that you also experience? It motivates you. You feel more a part of the group and less alone. that there is someone who shares your feelings. You had hope to move on because someone made the decision to be open and vulnerable. That is not at all weak; rather, it is strong. Being vulnerable is the best indicator of courage. Brave enough to appear and be seen even though we have no idea what is on the other side waiting for us. If we are brave enough, the physics of vulnerability dictates that we will stumble and fail. However, when we are courageous, we become better than when we choose to be weak and when we fail. We rise at this location and time. Either you'll choose bravery or comfort. Be assured, though, that you cannot have both. Comfortable seating in the arena to yell, shout, and have fun, or bravery to enter the arena to engage in combat, risk getting your ass kicked, and emerge victorious. You are living your life. Have the guts to own it.

What does being brave actually entail?

The saying "The more I learn, the less I know" is true when it comes to human behavior, emotions, and thought. I've come to realize that giving up on trying to capture certainty and secure it to a wall is best. There are even days when I miss feigning certainty. When I lock myself in my study and play songs David, my husband, always knows I'm lamenting the end of my young-researcher quest.Additionally, the manner he sings is just as important as the song's lyrics. He sometimes seems to be making fun of our arrogance in thinking we can ever know everything, and other times he seems angry that we can't. I feel better singing along in any case. I always feel less alone in the chaos when I listen to music. While there aren't any hard-and-fast rules in my industry, there are realities about common experiences that have a strong connection to what we know and believe. For instance, the Roosevelt quotation that serves as the foundation for my research on vulnerability and bravery gave rise to the following three facts for me: I desire a seat in the arena. I wish to live a daring life. And when we decide to dare tremendously, we voluntarily choose to have our asses kicked. We have a choice between comfort and boldness; we cannot have both. not simultaneously.

Having the guts to show up and be seen when we have no control over the outcome is what it means to be vulnerable; it has nothing to do with winning or losing. Our greatest sign of bravery is vulnerability, not strength. People who never step onto the floor are seated in many of the arena's inexpensive seats. They simply lob snide remarks and insults from a safe distance. The issue is that we lose our capacity to connect when we stop caring what other people think and stop being affected by harshness. But when we let other people's opinions define us, we stop being willing to be open and vulnerable. As a result, we must be careful about the feedback we allow into our lives. I personally am not interested in your feedback if you are not in the arena having you kicked.

Although I don't consider these to be "rules," they have undoubtedly evolved into my guiding principles. Before we begin the Rising process, I think it's helpful to understand some fundamental principles about being brave, taking risks, and overcoming adversity. These, in my opinion, are the fundamental principles of emotional physics. They are straightforward but profound facts that explain why courage is both rare and transformative. Four of the ten rules of engagement for rising strong are listed here.

1. When we decide to go and take the chance of falling, we are indeed deciding to fall. Saying "I'm willing to risk failure" is not being courageous. Daring is expressing the sentiment, "I know I'll fail eventually, but I'm still all in." Although failure also favors the brave, fortune might.

2. Once we give in to being fearless, there is no turning back. We can recover from our mistakes, missteps, and falls, but we can never return to the position in which we were before acting bravely or falling. Our emotional framework is altered by courage. This transition frequently causes a profound sense of loss. We may experience homesickness for a place that is no longer there when we are rising. There is no place to go back to when we wanted to, just before we entered the arena. We now have a higher level of awareness about what it means to be brave, which makes this more challenging. We can no longer pretend. Now, we are aware of when we are being present and when we are concealing, as well as when we are upholding our beliefs. Our new understanding can also be energizing since it can revive our feeling of purpose and serve as a reminder of our dedication to wholeheartedness. A necessary component of rising strong is juggling the tension that exists between

yearning for the time before we took a risk and fell and being propelled forward to even greater daring.

3. No one else is responsible for this journey but you, but no one has ever completed one on their own. Since the dawn of time, humans have discovered a method to get back up after falling, but there is no established route that leads there. We all have to choose our own paths, engaging in some of the most common activities while navigating a sense of isolation that gives us the impression that we are the first people to enter new territory. In addition, we must learn to rely on our fellow travelers for temporary shelter, support, and the occasional desire to walk beside them in place of the sense of security that comes from a well-trodden path or a frequent companion. Dealing with the solitude that is a necessary part of this process is a difficult challenge for those of us who are afraid of being alone. The demand for connection—asking for and accepting help—becomes the challenge for those of us who prefer to isolate ourselves from the world and recover alone.

4. Storytelling is in our DNA. There's a fairly straightforward reason we want to own, integrate, and share our experiences of difficulty in a society that values scarcity and perfection. We do this because it is biologically innate for us to feel most

alive when we are interacting with others and being courageous with our tales. The concept of storytelling has spread far. It serves as a platform for anything from marketing plans to creative movements. We're "wired for story," though, is more than just a catchphrase. In order to help us get back on our feet, I'm hoping that the Rising process will give us a vocabulary and a rough road map. I'm disclosing all that I understand about Rising brave, as well as how I feel, think, and experience it. I continue to be saved by what I learned from the research participants, and I am incredibly appreciative of that. Falling does hurt, that much is true. The challenge is to maintain your bravery and climb back up.

Accepting ourselves

In what sense should you "own your story"? In a nutshell, it refers to being open and honest with yourself about the good, the terrible, and the ugly aspects of your life. It entails refusing to invent tales to cover up mistakes or absolve oneself of responsibility. It also entails taking accountability for errors without taking ownership of things that aren't ours or giving in to shame. It entails accepting our humanness, accepting our flaws, learning from our mistakes, and working toward being more and more of who we were designed to be, rather than playing the victim or the hero role.

Saying "yes, this is a part of me" brings these things out of the shadows, forces us to face them, and gives us the option to choose a different course of action rather than denying or avoiding the fact that there are aspects of ourselves that we are not proud of in an effort to hide or avoid responsibility for them. What we conceal or deny cannot be changed. When we take ownership of our tales, they become redemptive. Redemption is the act of paying a price to obtain something back. The discomfort of examining your flaws or damaged spots for an extended period of time in order to heal and learn from them is the cost involved with this kind of redemption. The upside is that you may then include that chapter of your past into your present story without letting it consume you. When we deny our stories, they define us. We are never truly free when we flee conflict. Therefore, we face the truth and stare it in the eye. Our faults or flaws form chains around our hearts when we try to hide them, making it difficult for us to open up to others for fear that they may discover what we are hiding. I have worked as a therapist for about ten years, and throughout that time, I have repeatedly seen the strength of this phenomenon. Real vulnerability and connection happen when people are courageous enough to accept their flaws as chances for healing and development.

When we come to terms with the fact that we have locked our skeleton-filled closet from the inside, we have the ability to face our challenges head-on and work toward wholeness and genuine connection. I would advise you to start small if you are reading this and feeling like, "This sounds fantastic, but I have no idea where to start or how to achieve this." Find a reliable person—a counselor, a pastor, or a close friend—with whom you can discuss some of the aspects of your past that keep you up at night (or would, if you acknowledged them), and then give this person the freedom to say the truth and offer the support that comes with a hearty "me too" or "welcome to humanity." This is done to assist you experience the liberation of no longer allowing that decision or occurrence to bind you, not to lessen the severity of the perceived weakness or failing. Please get in touch with a therapist at Anthology if you are unable to find such a person; we would be pleased to assist you in starting this process.

The quake

A quake is a meeting, conversation, or discussion that is defined by the commitment to lean into vulnerability, to remain open-minded and kind, to stick with the messy middle of problem identification and solving, to take breaks and circle back when necessary, to own our parts fearlessly, and,to listen with the same fervor with which we want to be heard. In other words, a rumble is a meeting, conversation, or discussion that is characterized by these When I hear someone say, "Let's rumble," I know it's time to show up with an open heart and mind so that we can put the needs of the task and each other ahead of our own egos. In order to be courageous, we must keep our minds and hearts open. Always bear in mind that the thing that stands between you and bravery is armor, not fear. When we are fearful, we tend to start protecting ourselves, shutting down, and becoming more postured.

When I find myself going for my preferred piece of armor, I make it a point to remind myself that the antidote to arming up is to keep oneself engaged (perfectionism, wrath, being the knower, trying to control, emotional intensity, getting critical). If you're like the majority of people, you probably have an inaccurate conception of courage as an absence of fear. In point of fact, courage is defined as the capacity to act despite one's fear. The ability to take courageous action despite the presence of potential threats or worries is the essence of courage. Having an awareness of your anxieties and a determination not to be inhibited by them are two of the most effective methods to exhibit brave behavior. If you give it the chance, fear may stop you from moving forward in life, from taking chances, and from seizing opportunities when they present themselves. Being courageous, on the other hand, enables you to take risks, go for your goals, and accomplish the things you set out to do in your life. If you've been struggling with fear and want to feel more courageous in your life, there are various ways that you may build your courage muscles and get the most out of every situation. This article will provide you with a summary of the information you need to know about courage, as well as tips on how to ensure that your life is full of bravery.

The Benefits of Having Courage

If you have more courage in your life, you will be able to deal with risks more effectively and accomplish more in your lifetime. But you have to put in some work to conquer your worries. In point of fact, having courage means making decisions after thoughtfully weighing the potential downsides and upsides of those actions, and then acting despite the natural development of dread.

In addition to this, having bravery gives you the strength to work towards achieving your objectives. Your self-confidence will also rise, and it will become easier for you to believe in your own abilities. It is essential for you to comprehend that having courage does not equate to not being afraid.

Fear is a healthy emotion to have since it compels one to slow down, think things through, and be extra cautious around potentially harmful situations. Do not be hard on yourself or assume that you are weak because you are experiencing fear. Being able to take action despite feeling fear is an essential component of what it means to be courageous. In addition, the more you are able to confront your fears, the more frequently you will be able to replace your fear-based response with one that is based on courage. The following is a list of some additional benefits of having courage:

If you can demonstrate bravery in the face of fear, it may help you feel more confident.

Through the cultivation of courage, one might acquire a fresh viewpoint on the world.

People will have the tools they need to follow in your footsteps if they see you living a courageous life and learning from your example.

If you make the decision to push yourself outside your comfort zone and be more adventurous, you will become a more well-rounded person and broaden the range of experiences you have in life.

Being courageous pushes you to follow your goals and seize opportunities when they present themselves, which enhances the likelihood that you will achieve what you set out to do.

If you accept courage and make it a part of your life, you will find that your level of happiness increases.

How You Can Increase Your Boldness

Fear is a powerful emotion that has the potential to stifle forward movement. If you don't have the right perspective on fear, it might actually prevent you from taking chances and achieving the things you want to in life. As a consequence of this, many people choose to remain within their established routines out of fear rather than mustering the bravery to experiment with something novel despite the potential downsides.

If you believe that this scenario is quite similar to your life, you should examine it more carefully to determine the areas in which you could benefit from becoming more courageous. Do you have to actively seek that promotion at work, for instance, or can you just sit back and hope that they would notice your efforts? Or do you believe that the next time the bully at work insults someone, it is your responsibility to step in? There is a good chance that you will behave more courageously in a variety of settings during the course of your life. The following are some approaches that can assist you in embracing and putting courage to use in your life.

Maintain a Bright and Upbeat Attitude

Too frequently, people make the assumption that you were either born courageous or you weren't. And even while it's possible that some people are more likely to exhibit courage than others, this doesn't necessarily mean that everything is hopeless for you, even if it's possible that some people are more likely to show courage than others. 1 In point of fact, the best way to conceptualize courage is as a muscle. Even while some people may be born with muscles that are more defined than others, it is possible for everyone to grow stronger muscles of courage via the appropriate practice and training. It is essential to have the understanding that fear does not always have to be a negative feeling. Fear can be useful, but only in limited circumstances. Fear, for instance, triggers the survival instincts that are embedded in your nervous system and are designed to keep you safe in dangerous situations. As a result of this, you might feel dread whenever a stranger approaches you in a dark alley or whenever a tornado is raging outside. Rather than viewing your fear as a negative trait, think of it as an opportunity to learn more about who you are and the reasons why you might be wary of or less than thrilled about moving outside of your comfort zone. If you take the time to identify your fear and figure out why it's there, you might discover a better understanding of how to get over it or show courage in spite of it. In fact, studies show that verbalizing your emotions might reduce the detrimental effects of dread.

2 Speaking out about your anxieties also doesn't make you weak. It makes you braver, though. Since vulnerability must be acknowledged, it is not an easy task. Therefore, you will be one step closer to being courageous if you can admit your worries. As a result, acknowledge what is stopping you rather than downplaying or dismissing your fear. You are giving yourself the ability to be courageous despite feeling afraid by acknowledging your fear, whether by writing it down or by talking about it with a supporting person.

Find Your Strengths

When it comes to leading a courageous life, it can be helpful to start by recognizing your strengths and areas of accomplishment. In fact, research demonstrates that people who are aware of and build upon their talents are more resilient as well as happier and less unhappy.

3Additionally, knowing your strengths can raise your confidence, which increases your propensity for bravery and risk-taking. Likewise, when you have faith in your skills, you are far more likely to seize an opportunity when it arises. Additionally, it's normal to concentrate on your flaws and weaknesses while you are battling fear and wish to add more courage to your life. But doing this merely decreases your likelihood of feeling bold. For this reason, it's critical to consider your strengths as a strategy to boost your courage and confidence.

Examine Various Situations

When it comes to being courageous, it can be good to consider both the worst case scenario and the outcome if you took no action at all. Comparing the two extremes is frequently all you need to overcome your concerns because, most of the time, the worst case scenario is frequently insignificant in comparison to what you could stand to gain by taking action. If you employ comparisons like this frequently, you will eventually develop resistance to allowing your anxieties to govern you.

You might also conjure up situations in which you picture yourself undertaking a terrifying task. Imagine how you will handle each potential situation, including your various responses and statements. You can practice being brave with the help of these activities without having to put yourself in danger before you are ready.

Simple Steps for Beginning Guided Imagery Practice

Try to step outside of your comfort zone.

A life that isn't fully lived might happen when you allow fear to stop you from having fun, pursuing your dreams, or expressing your true self. And you'll need to live intentionally if you want to change that element of your life. You must force yourself to leave your comfort zone if you want to develop your courage muscles. Therefore, pick some situations where the risks are low but you feel uncomfortable. In other words, practice being brave by overcoming minor anxieties like dining alone in a restaurant or meeting new people before you take on something more difficult like taking the initiative on a project or organizing your neighborhood's toy drive. You can grow acclimated to being brave without taking many chances at first by starting small. You will eventually reach a stage where you can accept greater risks.

Become less stressed

Exhaustion and the prospect of taking on any additional tasks that appear to be too challenging can frequently be the source of feelings of dread or a lack of bravery. If you find that you are feeling overburdened, frazzled, or bogged down, you should look for ways to reduce the stress that you are experiencing. When you are under a lot of pressure, it can be hard to maintain your bravery. Consider the options available to you so that you can reduce the amount of stress in your life. In addition to taking care of yourself, find ways to relax and decompress in your free time. Because of this, it may occasionally be necessary to go on a short vacation or take some much-needed time off from work. Everyone requires a break every once in a while. If the thought of working on being more courageous causes you to feel like you can't handle it, then the first step you need to take is to find ways to reduce the amount of stress in your life.

Salute Courageous Deeds

Each and every courageous deed deserves commendation, but especially so if it is something that the person has never done before. Remember the times in your life when you overcame your fears and behaved boldly, and don't let them slip your mind. It is essential to give yourself praise and recognise the effort that was required in order to confront your anxieties. In point of fact, the majority of professionals are in agreement that those who acknowledge and place importance on even the smallest of successes are more likely to have sustained success.

Keep a mental record of your accomplishments and give yourself permission to feel proud of them. Obviously, you don't need to announce it loudly or post it on social media, but you should keep a record of them nonetheless. You might even want to make a record of these short affirmations so that you can look back on them if you're feeling sad or like you're lacking boldness in your life. This will allow you to refer to them whenever you need to. Because of this, you won't have the opportunity to entertain negative thoughts or the presumption that you will never be courageous.

Acceptable Failure

The majority of individuals are frightened of failure, which is one of the primary reasons why they regularly do nothing. In point of fact, people who are frightened of failing may adopt rigid standards and a perfectionist attitude in an effort to avoid the embarrassment or shame that comes along with failing. This is done in an effort to escape the embarrassment or shame that comes along with failing.

Failure, on the other hand, presents an opportunity for growth and should be embraced. Remind yourself that it's alright to fail, especially if you tried something new or pushed yourself outside of your comfort zone in order to succeed.

In the end, falling short of one's goals gives an opportunity for one's own growth. It presents you with the opportunity to widen your horizons, select a different path, and learn about the potential that lies inside yourself. In addition, if you choose to view it as a wonderful experience rather than the worst possible consequence, this will drive you to take risks and try out new things. When it comes to having the guts to do what's right, it's never too late to start living a life of adventure. In point of fact, bravery is simply another trait that, like any other, may be developed via life experience and conscious effort. It is merely a matter of having the strength of will to recognize your concerns and the intestinal fortitude to choose to act in spite of them.

When you are aware of your fears and take preventative measures to address them in order to achieve your objectives, you will not only experience an increase in your level of self-confidence but also an increase in your overall level of productivity. If you view your fears as an opportunity to build your courage muscles, you will eventually be able to push past your discomfort and lead the kind of life you have always sought. This will happen if you use your problems as an opportunity.

The uprising

It might not feel like it could be that way, but it's true that you can learn how to transform your life and fulfill the dreams you've always had.

If you take the time to look about, you will find that there is always someone in the world who grew up in the same area, time, and situation as you did, but who was able to make positive changes in their life.

However, just because you have the ability to make changes in your life does not indicate that doing so will be simple. I've lost count of the number of times that significant shifts have occurred in my life. And regardless of whether I was shifting my viewpoint, switching careers, or moving to a new country, I always came back to the same conclusion: If I wanted to make a genuine difference in my life, I needed to start by making changes in myself.

It's easier to say than it is to actually accomplish, right?

Nevertheless, if you are interested in becoming more self-motivated, being your own boss, or, you know, moving to Italy, learning Italian, falling in love, and opening a restaurant, then this is the path for you.

A Guide to Making Changes in Your Life

1. Make the Conscious Choice to Alter Your Life

It is possible that this is the most challenging aspect of making changes in your life, despite the fact that it may sound straightforward. While I've been traveling, I've had a lot of conversations with folks who have told me that they want to make substantial life changes, but they just can't seem to get it together to do it. Why is that? Simply because it's not easy to make big changes in your life. Extremely challenging. In point of fact, making significant changes in your life can be the single most difficult and unsettling thing you've ever done. A buddy of mine had an epiphany in which they exclaimed, "Oh my God - if I want to change my life, I have to change my life," and it was a profound moment for both of them. At first, this could make you feel very uneasy.

Depending on the reasons you desire to make a change in your life, you might find that following your aspirations requires you to relocate to a city or nation where you have no friends or family. It's possible that in order to make room for new friendships, you'll have to break some long-standing relationships first. Alternately, you might have to give up a secure job in favor of the unpredictable rollercoaster that is running your own business.,To put it another way, if you want to change your life, you have to make some difficult choices. To what extent do you want to alter the course of your life? And what are you prepared to sacrifice in order to make it a reality, both in terms of time and resources? When you make the decision to improve your life no matter what, suddenly you open the door to a world of possibilities.

Step 2: Become Accustomed to Being Uncomfortable

If you want to understand how to make a significant change in your life, you must be willing to leave the safety and security of your comfort zone. Moving beyond what one has experienced in the past is the essential component of personal development. You will have to explore uncharted territory. Life will only change when you become more committed to your aspirations than you are to your comfort zone. Therefore, make it a habit to challenge yourself and move outside of your safety zone whenever the opportunity presents itself. Take, for instance:

Avoid placing a second order of the same dish.

Take in music from a wide variety of genres.

Watching documentaries can really open your eyes.

Participate in a physical contest by signing up for it.

Change your driving habits on the way back.

Send a message to a person you haven't talked to in many years.

Always be willing to adapt to new circumstances.

Step 3: Determine the Reasons Behind Your Desire to Make Changes in Your Life

When trying to figure out how to make changes in your life, it is frequently simpler to begin by deciding what you do not want before moving on to consider what it is that you do want. Therefore, make a list of the areas of your life that you find to be unsatisfactory.

Do you despise the work that you do? Do you have a lot of negative feelings about the place you live, the people in your life, or how you generally feel? Do you want to break free from any detrimental routines or conditions in your life? Don't let yourself get caught up in the gloom and doom by ruminating on these things. Simply put them in writing and move on to the next phase as soon as possible.

Outline the Alterations You Would Like to Implement

It's time to start thinking outside the box: how do you want to make changes in your life? Perhaps you'd like to:

Launch your own company.

Change your residence to a new area.

Alter your profession.

Go traveling

Make new buddies

Try out a brand-new pastime.

Put the past in the past.

Put an end to your procrastination.

Develop your self-assurance.

Maintain a consistent pattern in the morning.

Regardless of what it is, as soon as you think of an idea, there may be a voice in your head that gives you all the reasons why your idea is "dumb," "unrealistic," or "will never work." This voice may tell you that your idea is "stupid," "unrealistic," or "will never work."

Don't give in to the pressure of that voice. This is a voice that is resistant to change. The possibilities are endless. Consider what Madonna has to say about the subject: "No matter who you are, no matter what you did, and no matter where you've come from, you can always change and become a better version of yourself."

5. Identify the Obstacles that may prevent you from achieving your goals.

The next step is to pinpoint any routines, mental patterns, or persons in your life that can prevent you from implementing positive changes in your life. Take, for example:

Do you procrastinate?

Do you have a problem with your relationship with sugar, alcohol, social media, pornography, or gaming?

Do you constantly criticize and berate yourself in your head?

Exist in your life persons who are always finding fault and discouraging you from making an effort?

If you are having trouble identifying the obstacles that could prevent you from making positive changes in your life, you should think about enlisting the assistance of a trusted close friend or member of your own family.

Always keep an eye out for trouble spots, even before they materialize. Again, it's important not to get caught up in the negative aspects of the situation; instead, jot them down and move on to the next stage.

Choose your "one thing" as the sixth step.

When you are trying to figure out how to make significant changes in your life, it is essential to keep in mind that this is a process that takes time; the changes won't take place all at once. If you try to make too many changes all at once, you will most likely become overwhelmed, experience burnout, and then revert to your typical style of conducting business. Therefore, tackle one challenge at a time. This is what you should do: Put your attention on a single major transition, such as relocating to a new place or switching employment. Or you could focus on breaking just one "keystone habit." In an arch, the centre stone, known as the keystone, is responsible for holding all of the other stones together. The formation of keystone behaviors fosters the development of other habits that are related.

www.ingramcontent.com/pod-product-compliance
Lightning Source LLC
Chambersburg PA
CBHW050326220526
45465CB00005B/2144